# Dream It, Do It!

# GET INVENTING!

Mary Colson

Raintree

Chicago, Illinois

To contact Capstone Global Library please phone 800-747-4992, or visit
our web site www.capstonepub.com

Edited by Rebecca Rissman, Dan Nunn, and Helen Cox Cannons
Designed by Steve Mead
Original illustrations © Capstone Global Library, Ltd
Picture research by Ruth Blair
Production by Vicki Fitzgerald
Originated by Capstone Global Library, Ltd
Printed and bound in China by CTPS

17 16 15 14 13
10 9 8 7 6 5 4 3 2 1

**Library of Congress Cataloging-in-Publication Data**
Colson, Mary, author.
  Get inventing! / Mary Colson.
       pages cm.—(Dream it, do it!)
Includes bibliographical references and index.
ISBN 978-1-4109-6264-5 (hb)—ISBN 978-1-4109-6269-0 (pb)  1.
Inventions—Juvenile literature. 2. Technology—Juvenile literature. 3.
Children as inventors—Juvenile literature.  I. Title.

T48.C62 2014
600—dc23                              2013017424

**Acknowledgments**
The author and publisher are grateful to the following for permission
to reproduce copyright material: Capstone Publishers pp. 21, 26–29
(all © Karon Dubke); FLPA p. 23 (Nicholas and Sherry Lu Aldridge);
Getty Images pp. 5 (MJ Kim), 24 (Hulton Archive); Shutterstock pp. 6 (©
Africa Studio), 7 (© Christopher Edwin Nuzzaco), 8 left (© Rob Byron), 8
right (© colorvsbw), 9 (© Edwin Verin), 11 top (© IM_photo), 11 bottom
(© Zurijeta), 12 left (© Vorobyeva), 12 middle (© Cherkas), 12 bottom
(© Sergiy Telesh); 13 (© fabio fersa), 14 (© Jason Vandehey), 15 (©
Poznyakov), 16 (© Monkey Business Images), 17 (© Kamil Macniak),
18 (© ffolas), 19 (© Ivonne Wierink), 20 (© wawritto), 22 (© djem), 25
(© Andrey_Kuzmin), 25 (© Stocksnapper). Incidental photographs
reproduced with permission of Shutterstock.

Cover photograph of a woman flying reproduced with permission of
Getty Images (Westend61).

# CONTENTS

Some words are shown in bold, **like this**. You can find out what they mean by looking in the glossary.

# BE AN INVENTOR!

Take a look around you. Many of the things that you can see were invented. From the wheels on your bicycle to the television in your house, an inventor dreamed them up and brought their ideas to life. Inventors are **curious** and imaginative people. If you dream of inventing new machines and **gadgets**, then dream big!

## Inspiration

Get yourself a notebook and start your own "Inventor's Secret **Journal**." Write down all of your wonderful ideas!

# GETTING GREAT IDEAS

Inventors are always on the lookout for new ideas. They try to improve everyday objects that we already have, or they create brand new things.

Cut out pictures from magazines of inventions that you like. The pictures can show small things, such as kitchen **utensils**, or big things, such as cars. Stick the pictures in your **journal**. Write down what it is about the objects that works well. Think about how you could improve them.

# IMPROVING WHAT'S THERE

Most inventions are improvements on existing items or ways of doing things. For example, if a tool or **utensil** doesn't work as well as it should, an inventor will think about how to improve it.

Think about the objects that you use in the hobbies and activities in your life. Can you think of any ways in which the objects could be improved?

# TACKLING PROBLEMS

Inventors need time, patience, and open minds to make their inventions work. They also need to respond to what people suggest or advise. For example, the airplane was invented after a lot of practice, changes, and experiments.

## Activity

Invent a new type of flying machine, and draw it in your inventor's **journal**. What shape will the machine be? What **fuel** will it use? What will it be made of?

You can't actually try out your flying machine, but you can ask friends to look at your design. Can they see any problems with it?

# TESTING MATERIALS

Inventors work with all kinds of materials, such as wood, plastic, steel, and brick. They think about which materials will be best for the object's purpose. After all, it's no use making a teapot out of chocolate!

Imagine that you're going to invent a new type of boat. First, you will need to test out some materials. Try floating different materials in your bathtub to see which will be best for your invention. **Review** your floating test. Which was the best material for your boat? Why?

# INVENTOR'S STUDIO

Most inventors have a studio, or space, where they do their most top-secret work. Some inventors work in **laboratories**, and some even work underground.

Create a space where you can sit, think, and write down ideas. You will need pens, paper, and your inventor's **journal**. Make sure your space is safe from pets and younger brothers or sisters!

# HELPING OTHERS

Inventors work to make life easier for everybody. Imagine a machine that cleaned your bedroom in five minutes!

# Activity

Ask people in your family about what they would find useful. A new type of **utensil** for cooking? A **gadget** to pick up slippery spaghetti? A duster that reaches the top shelf? Think about what the object would be used for and how you would make it work.

# COOKING UP A TREAT!

Did you know that you can invent new recipes? Chefs are always thinking creatively to invent new and tasty dishes.

# Activity

In your inventor's **journal**, draw some cupcakes with some new toppings. Remember to label your cupcakes with the **ingredients** and flavors that you would use. Why not try some unusual flavors and colors?

With an adult's help, make cupcakes to test out your ideas using different ingredients for toppings. You might be surprised by what works! Get your family to taste test your cupcakes.

# ECO-INVENTIONS

Modern inventors often try to recycle objects and make them into new, usable items. Can you think of something new to make from an object that you would usually throw away?

# Activity

In your inventor's studio, take a plastic food tray, some paper, sticky tape or glue, and pens. Make this into a new object, such as a desk organizer. Think about what the finished object has to do.

Did your invention work? Could it be improved? Write down your findings in your inventor's **journal**.

# WATER-WISE INVENTIONS

An important issue for the inventors of today and tomorrow is using **natural resources**, such as water, wisely.

Water meter

# Activity

Invent an object that collects rainwater, which can be used to water indoor plants. You could use plastic from your recycling box at home.

What worked and what didn't work? Did you get enough water for your plants? Make notes in your inventor's **journal**, and think about how you could improve your invention.

Rain catcher

# PRACTICE MAKES PERFECT!

Not all inventions work right away, or even at all. Even inventors need to practice inventing! Famous inventors such as Thomas Edison, who invented the lightbulb, created lots of things that worked but many more that didn't.

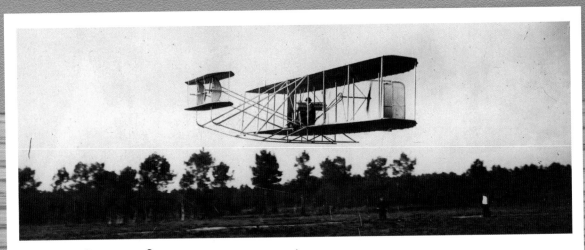

One of the first ever airplanes, invented by the Wright brothers.

## Activity

Look back through your inventor's **journal**. Which of your inventions was most successful? Is there a particular invention that you want to develop? Which one do you think could make the most difference in people's lives?

Try making that idea out of different materials. Can you improve on what you've already done?

# GAME MASTER!

Every year, inventors carefully plan and create exciting new toys and games for people to enjoy. Imagine that a toy company has asked you to invent a new board game for a family to play. Follow these simple steps to help you get started:

1. In your inventor's **journal**, write down the purpose of the game. Is it to win money or property? Is it to be first to go around the board?

2. How many players will your game be for?

3. How do players move around the board? Do they roll dice?

4. Think about the board's design. What does it look like?

5. What will stop a player from winning? What are the traps?

6. Do you need to write **forfeit cards**?

7. Do you need to design game money or tokens?

8. How will you know who is the winner?

Explain the rules of your game to friends. Play the game together. Did they suggest any improvements? Does the board design work?

# GLOSSARY

**curious**  wanting to know things

**forfeit card**  card that forces someone to give up something in a board game

**fuel**  energy or power, such as gasoline

**gadget**  small tool with a clever design

**ingredients**  food items in a recipe

**journal**  written record of a person's thoughts and experiences

**laboratory**  place used for scientific testing

**natural resources**  materials that are found in nature, such as coal, wood, and water

**review**  look back at something that has already taken place and see what went right or wrong

**utensil**  cooking tool

# FIND OUT MORE

## Books

Enz, Tammy. *Invent It!* (series). Mankato, Minn: Capstone, 2012.

Spengler, Kremena T. *An Illustrated Timeline of Inventions and Inventors.* Mankato, Minn.: Picture Window, 2012.

## Web sites

FactHound offers a safe, fun way to find Internet sites related to this book. All of the sites on FactHound have been researched by our staff.

Here's all you do:

Visit www.facthound.com

Type in this code: 9781410962645

# INDEX